Diving Dolphin

Written by Karen Wallace

Series Editor Deborah Lock
Project Editor Caryn Jenner
Art Editors Jane Horne, Rashika Kachroo
US Editors Regina Kahney, Shannon Beatty
Managing Editor Soma B. Chowdhury
Managing Art Editor Ahlawat Gunjan
Production Editor Marc Staples
DTP Designer Anita Yadav
Picture Researchers Angela Anderson, Sumedha Chopra
Jacket Designers Natalie Godwin, Martin Wilson
Publishing Manager Bridget Giles
Art Director Martin Wilson
Natural History Consultant Theresa Greenaway

Reading Consultant
Linda Gambrell, Ph.D.

First American Edition, 2001, 2011
This edition, 2015
15 16 17 18 19 10 9 8 7 6 5 4 3 2 1
001—270537—June/15

Published in the United States by DK Publishing
345 Hudson Street, 4th Floor
New York, New York 10014

DK books are available at special discounts when purchased in bulk for sales promotions, premiums, fund-raising, or
educational use. For details, contact: DK Publishing Special Markets, 345 Hudson Street, 4th Floor, New York,
New York 10014 or SpecialSales@dk.com.

A catalog record for this book is available from the Library of Congress
ISBN: 978-1-4654-2829-5 (paperback)
ISBN: 978-1-4654-3020-5 (hardback)

Printed and bound in China

The publisher would like to thank the following for their kind permission to reproduce their images:
Position key: c=center; b=bottom; l=left; r=right; t=top
Bruce Coleman Ltd: Jeff Foott 22-23; **N.H.P.A.:** 30-31, 33c; Gerrard Lacz 8-9, 19, 43bl; Kevin Schafer 32; **Planet Earth
Pictures:** Ken Lucas 10-11; **Telegraph Colour Library:** 6-7, 7b; David Fleetham 34-35, 39t; David Nardina 11tr; Doug
Perrine 24, 25, 26, 38, 41; Gnadinger 18b, 27t; John Seagrim 39b; Masterfile 40; Peter Scoones 16-17; Planet Earth/James D
Watt, 43bl; Steve Bloom 14-15, 25; **123RF.com:** Anastasy Yarmolovich 1b; **Alamy Images:** FLPA 42br, David Noble
4-5 (Background), 20-21 (Background), 28-29 (Background), 36-37 (Background), Radius Images 36-37, blickwinkel/
Schmidbauer 28-29; **Corbis:** 42cla, Dave Fleetham/Design Pics 5tl, Tong Guoqiang/Xinhua Press 5bl, Image Source 13clb,
Flip Nicklin/Minden Pictures 5cl; **Dreamstime.com:** Winai Tepsuttinun 20l, 21ca; **Fotolia:** Karl Bolf 13tl; **Getty Images:**
Eisenhut and Mayer Wien/Photolibrary 12cr, Tom Brakefield/Digital Vision 42bl, Tom Brakefield/Stockbyte 4cb, M Swiet
Productions/Moment 42cra; **Science Photo Library:** Wim Van Egmond/Visuals Unlimited, Inc 13crb
Jacket images: *Front:* **Getty Images:** Mike Hill / Photographer's Choice.
Back: **Getty Images:** David Nardini / Taxi cra.
All other images © Dorling Kindersley.
For further information see : www.dkimages.com

A WORLD OF IDEAS:
SEE ALL THERE IS TO KNOW
www.dk.com

Contents

I'm Not a Fish!

Dolphins are mammals and not fish. Here are some differences between dolphins and fish.

Dolphins   # Fish

Covered in smooth,
slippery skin

Covered in
overlapping scales

Breathe through
a blowhole

Breathe using
their gills

Give birth
to live young

Many lay eggs

A young dolphin
dives through the water.
His shiny skin is
as smooth as satin.
Far below,
he sees his mother.

6

His baby sister
swims beside her mother.

The young dolphin twirls
beside his mother.
Their flippers touch.
They rub each other's beaks.

Where has the
baby dolphin gone?

Mother dolphin calls her baby.
She makes a special
whistling sound.

Whistle!
Whistle!

The baby hears her mother calling.
The baby turns and
stays beside her.

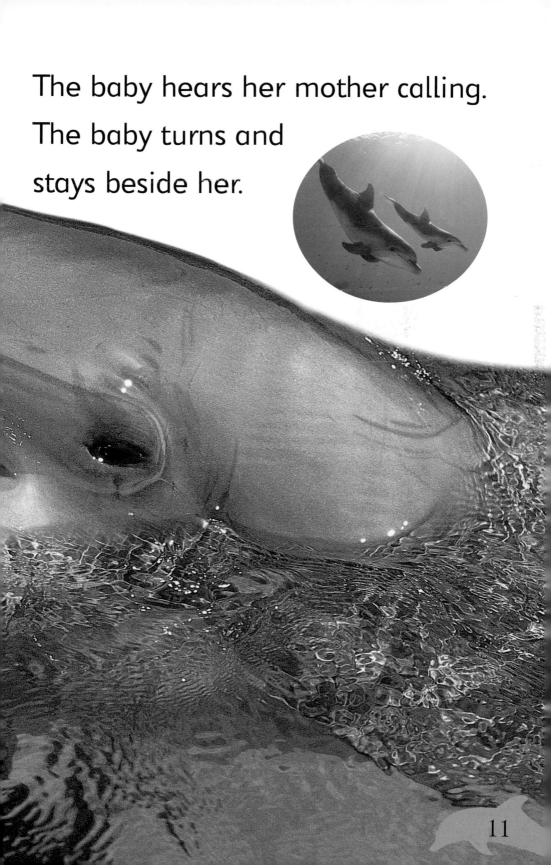

Ocean Café

Welcome, dolphins! All food comes from your local area.

Fish

herring

cod

mackerel

mullet

catfish

flounder

gobies

carp

anchovy

Served stunned by tail, rubbed on the ocean floor, shaken, or stripped into pieces.

Special dishes

squid

jellyfish

shrimp

Side orders

small shellfish

plankton

seaweed

No chewing allowed!
Swallow whole for best results!

The young dolphin swims away
with older dolphins.
He leaves his mother
and his baby sister.

He twirls and leaps
with the older dolphins.
They splash the water
with their tails.

15

Hundreds of fish
flash through the water.
The fish turn together.

The dolphins follow.
The frightened fish
swim around in circles.

Dolphins snatch the silver fish.
Their teeth are sharp.
They gulp the fish down whole.

The growing dolphin
is always hungry.
He eats and eats to fill his belly.

Make Waves

You will need:

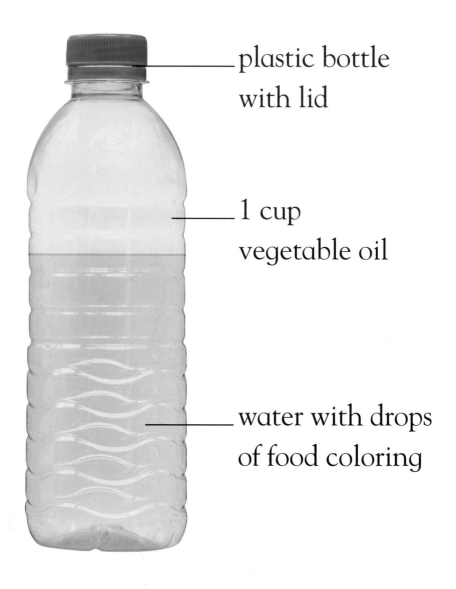

plastic bottle
with lid

1 cup
vegetable oil

water with drops
of food coloring

What to do:

Tip the bottle back and forth
to make some waves.

Watch!

The water just moves up
and down. The waves
travel through
the water.

The dolphins turn
and dive together.
They spin and tumble.

They squeal and whistle.
When one swims off
the others follow.

23

The young dolphin
roams the ocean.
He hunts for fish through
beds of seaweed.

He rides the waves
to travel faster.
The waves push him
over the sparkling water.

The dolphin leaps
as the sun is setting.
The sea is smooth
and fish are hiding.

The dolphin sees the fish
in the water.
They glow like stars
far beneath him.

27

Killer Whale Close-up

A killer whale is
the biggest dolphin.
It is also called an orca.

saddle patch

belly patch

fluke

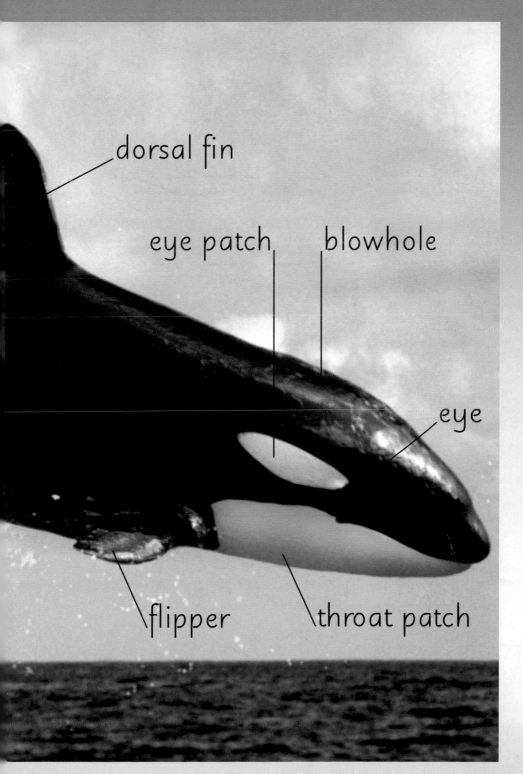

dorsal fin

eye patch   blowhole

eye

flipper   throat patch

29

The dolphin chases
the fish.
He swims down and down
to the sandy seabed.

He does not know
that killer whales
watch him from above.
The killer whales are hungry.

The killer whales
shoot through the water.
Their jaws are strong.
Their teeth are like knives.

The young dolphin
gives a warning whistle.
The other dolphins
race away.

The killer whales
swim through the water.
The dolphins hear them
coming closer.

The young dolphin hides.

He makes no sound.

This time the killer whales

don't find him.

Dolphin Boat Tours

Join the Dolphin Boat Tours.
Watch dolphins live!
Marvel at their dazzling moves
right before your eyes.
A must-see display as
they twist and turn together!

Don't miss out!
Monday–Saturday
10 AM and 2 PM

Reserve your
spot today!

The dolphin leaps.
He breathes in air
through a blowhole
on the top of
his head.

The dolphin dives again.

A turtle watches him.

An octopus waggles past
through the water.

Now the young dolphin
swims back to his mother.
His baby sister
has grown bigger.
Their flippers touch.
They rub each other's beaks.

Soon the dolphin
will hunt for fish again.

Pod Photos

Dolphins live, work, and play together.
Their groups are called pods.

Swimming races!
Dolphins travel together.

Family time!
Dolphins protect each other.

Having fun!
Dolphins leap and dive together.

Feeding time!
Dolphins work together to catch fish.

42

Diving Dolphin Quiz

1. What is a group of dolphins called?

2. What did the dolphins catch?

3. What did the dolphin hide from?

4. What warning sound did the dolphins make?

5. Name these parts:

 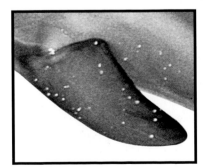

Answers on page 45.

Glossary

beak mouth part of a dolphin used for grabbing food

blowhole hole on a dolphin's head used for breathing in and out

dorsal fin tall, triangle-shape fin on a dolphin's back

flipper front limb of a dolphin used for steering as it swims

fluke one of the parts of a whale's tail

gills breathing part of a fish

jaw bony part of the mouth that holds the teeth

scales bony plates that cover a fish's skin

Index

Answers to the Diving Dolphin Quiz:
1. Pod; **2.** Fish; **3.** Killer whales;
4. Whistle; **5.** Blowhole, flipper.

Guide for Parents

DK Readers is a four-level interactive reading adventure series for children, developing the habit of reading widely for both pleasure and information. These books have an exciting main narrative interspersed with a range of reading genres to suit your child's reading ability, as required by the Common Core State Standards. Each book is designed to develop your child's reading skills, fluency, grammar awareness, and comprehension in order to build confidence and engagement when reading.

Ready for a *Beginning to Read* book

YOUR CHILD SHOULD

- be familiar with using beginning letter sounds and context clues to figure out unfamiliar words.
- be aware of the need for a slight pause at commas and a longer one at periods.
- alter his/her expression for questions and exclamations.

A VALUABLE AND SHARED READING EXPERIENCE

For many children, reading requires much effort, but adult participation can make this both fun and easier. So here are a few tips on how to use this book with your child.

TIP 1 Check out the contents together before your child begins:

- read the text about the book on the back cover.
- flip through the book and and stop to chat about the contents page together to heighten your child's interest and expectation.
- make use of unfamiliar or difficult words on the page in a brief discussion.
- chat about the non-fiction reading features used in the book, such as headings, captions, recipes, lists or charts.

TIP 2 Support your child as he/she reads the story pages:

- give the book to your child to read and turn the pages.

- where necessary, encourage your child to break a word into syllables, sound out each one, and then flow the syllables together. Ask him/her to reread the sentence to check the meaning.

- when there's a question mark or an exclamation mark, encourage your child to vary his/her voice as he/she reads the sentence. Demonstrate how to do this if it is helpful.

TIP 3 Chat at the end of each page:

- the factual pages tend to be more difficult than the story pages, and are designed to be shared with your child.

- ask questions about the text and the meaning of the words used. These help to develop comprehension skills and awareness of the language used.

A FEW ADDITIONAL TIPS

- Always encourage your child to try reading difficult words by themselves. Praise any self-corrections, for example, "I like the way you sounded out that word and then changed the way you said it, to make sense."

- Try to read together everyday. Reading little and often is best. These books are divided into manageable chapters for one reading session. However, after 10 minutes, only keep going if your child wants to read on.

- Read other books of different types to your child just for enjoyment and information.

Series consultant, **Dr. Linda Gambrell**, Distinguished Professor of Education at Clemson University, has served as President of the National Reading Conference, the College Reading Association, and the International Reading Association. She is also reading consultant for the **DK Adventures**.

Have you read these other great books from DK?

BEGINNING TO READ

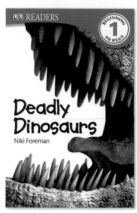

Roar! Thud! Meet the dinosaurs. Who do you think is the deadliest?

Holly's dream has come true— she gets her very own puppy.

Hard hats on! Watch the busy machines build a new school.

BEGINNING TO READ ALONE

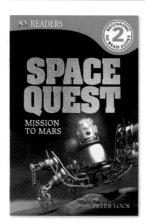

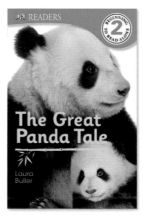

Embark on a mission to explore the solar system. First stop—Mars.

Join Louise at the zoo, preparing to welcome a new panda baby.

Discover life in a medieval castle during peacetime and war.